UNDER THE SHADOW OF HIS WINGS

BY

CRYSTAL A. HINDERER

Dedication & Thank you

I would like to thank Lindsey Kavis, Dan Chamberlain, Craig Swanson, Jackie Davis, Stan & Mary Wilhelm, Mike Burman and Rick Harris for their time and personal help to me along the way. It has meant more than they know.

Thank you to the gals at the Koontz Lake Library for their time and patience.

To Pastor Doug Jividen and Pastor Jim Repp from the Plymouth Baptist Church for their encouragement, help, and prayers.

To Jeri Carlson for her valued insight, research, and direction to Xulon Publishers and her prayers.

To Xulon Publishers for offering my husband and I the opportunity to publish our first book.

And to my husband Butch of 35 years for giving me the precious gift of time to write. He not only encourages me, but often tells me "God speaks through your pen." I may write the stories, but I could not do what I do without the time Butch has provided for me. This is truly our ministry together and I am so thankful for what we share. I thank God often for Butch, my husband, brother in Christ, and my best friend. I am so blessed and I love you so.

Crystal A. Hinderer

Preface

There is a God, the Living God, and all one has to do to find God is to seek Him. And if anyone wants to hear Him all they have to do is learn to listen. God speaks in so many ways. He speaks through the voices of people in word or song, The Holy Bible, and on lines of ink of others. But make no mistake, God speaks. And if you truly seek God He will be found, and He will even answer.

As I write, I am thinking of just what is the essence of what I write and why? What I want others to see is Christ the Savior and God, and His hand still at work in the world today. For people to focus more deeply on God. To know His presence is real, and that God is the Living god, not just the God "heard of" in stories long ago, but the God of here and now. I want people to feel what I write. No, there is no audible voice, or hand writing on the wall, but like a gentle breeze you cannot see, yet you know it is there, I hear God undeniably speak.

I pray you hear Him

Crystal A. Hinderer

TABLE OF CONTENTS

A Most Precious Gift

We all have 24 hours in a day. I heard this idea explained on a radio program once. The person was trying to get the point a crossed that we each have the same amount of time to work with each day. I argued with that idea years ago in my mind when I first heard it, and I still argue with it today. For yes we all have 24 hours in a day; but we do not all have the same time.

One cannot compare a mother with children to a wife with no children. There are people who must care for invalid parents, or a child with handicaps, or an injured spouse. These all may need 24 hour care.

My husband in June of 1999 gave me the gift of being home. I told him it was the most precious gift he could have ever given me. I worked the last fourteen and a half years of our 28-year marriage out of the house, and now I am able to be home again. When our son and daughter were in 3rd and 5th grades I had to go to work to help. I disliked being out of the house but my helpmate needed help. He is a good man that I love very much.

I have been more thankful and appreciative of my husband in 28 years than not. Thankful for days home, thankful for what we have, and learned to be thankful for the have-nots. I learned to do without necessities at times, learned to make do; and I have prayed through the years for my husband to grow spiritually. But God gave me a new twist on my thinking just the other day. While I have been truly thankful in many areas over the years, in other areas I have been frustrated and negative in thinking, "will he ever grow?" God let me see that yes I read, pray, and study the Word, but my husband is the one who has made it possible for me to have the time to read, pray, and study.

Even at 28 years of marriage my husband usually works 12-14 hour shifts, and drives one-hour to work and one-hour home 6 times a week. He does not have much time to sleep or be home, or even enjoy the yard. I cried when this sank in, because at what a great price he sacrifices for me, and has done so for 28 years. Sacrificing his growth for mine, by sacrificing his time for mine.

In a way I can see my husband in the story of the widow's mite, concerning his time in the same way. Some have abundance and can give more easily, while others give out of their daily living. While I have been growing "spiritually", wondering if he will ever grow; he is busy putting love into action truly following Christ in giving of himself daily.
Lord help me to grow spiritually.

By Crystal A. Hinderer

Proverbs 31:12 "She will do him good and not evil all the days of her life."

Back To Reality

All my life I have heard people say after a weekend away, or on nearing the end of some free time, "now back to reality"; as if in a dream world, and every day life is the only thing real.

But I began to think how the every day life of living in this world and family all tug at us. There are so many" tugs" in just the every day busyness of life. When we go to our private place, our closet, to stop and be alone with God, it seems we are leaving the reality of the busyness of life, and entering the Reality of God.

The very things we see, to exist in, in the reality of life, are the very things we need to hold loosely for the Reality of God; when we seek God and pray in a quiet place with Him alone. Away from the cares of this life and world, alone with God. Even away from our loved ones to give God our undivided attention, to put God first. Faith in God and prayer goes beyond what we can see, or feel, or fully understand through life in this world of reality.

For God's Reality changes hearts, touches lives, reconciles hurts, restores anew, reinforces our faith, and heals mental wounds as nothing else can. The Reality of God reaches far beyond what any reality of this life could ever imagine, or dream, or hope, or be. God's Reality is beyond all measure of what we can only try to fathom.

God will answer prayers in remarkable ways in His timing, and carry you through this life in ways that could only be His wisdom.

When truly seeking the only real God, He will capture you. He will be your reality of expectation, and your exceeding great reward.

By Crystal A. Hinderer

Psalms 62:5 "My soul wait thou only upon God, for my expectation is from Him."

Jer. 33:3 "Call unto me, and I will answer thee, and show thee great and mighty things which thou knowest not."

Prov. 24; 14 "So shall the knowledge of wisdom be unto thy soul, when thou hast found it, then there shall be a reward and they expectation shall not be cut off."

My Drink Of Water

The early morning hours are my favorite. I enjoy that time of day very much, I have all my life. I like the sunshine, the stillness in the darkness, the quiet before the world gets busy as if the whole world were sleeping; and the gradual awakening of the day when the sun is barely seen.

I also like walking at daybreak, and talking to The Almighty, The One who gave us this earth to use while we are here. While walking I often see bunnies, deer, and a whooping crane that stops at a near by creek. I enjoy the fresh air and being out. I'm a get-up and get-going person. I love those walks!

I thank God I am blessed to have the health to even be able to walk, and eyes to see the beauty of the earth; and for the precious gift of time.

Is it wrong to walk in the morning? No not at all, but I know me. And I know how busy my day can become. If I do not take time for God first, I may not get another opportunity.

My walks with God are precious, but the fellowship God and I share alone is of the greatest reward to me. (Prov. 3:9) "Honor the Lord with thy substance, and with the first fruits of all thine increase." My increase right now is time, and I need to put God first. I need to discipline me, to seek God with undivided attention. God is also a jealous God. (Ex. 20:13) "Thou shalt have no other God's before me." Not even nature, or walking.

Someone shared in Sunday school that we should give God what He deserves, not what's left over. I need to remember that always.

In 2 Samuel 23:15-16 and 1 Chronicles 11:17-19 David longed for a drink of water from the well of Bethlehem, which is by the gate. David's three mighty men risked their lives through Philistine lines to bring David some water from the well. But David would not drink of if, but poured it out to the Lord.

When I give up walking the first thing in the morning, it is like pouring out my drink of water to God. It is my gift to Him. God's desire is only for our best, and "God gives the best to those who let him choose" I have heard it said. I want God to choose for me every day. One of my prayers I often pray is, God, never let me let you go.

By Crystal A. Hinderer

Math. 5:6 "Blessed are they which do hunger and thirst after righteousness; for they shall be filled."

John 4:14 "But whoso drinketh of the water that I shall give him shall never thirst; but the water that I shall give him shall be in him a well of water springing up into everlasting life."

9-11

We keep hearing the question "Has your life changed since 9-11?" There has been much chatter over the last year. People get into conversations about air travel, the economy, terrorists, and war.

Has your life changed since 9-11? I've given this a lot of thought, and so I ask myself. Has my life changed since 9-11? Do I live differently since that day? I've come to the conclusion that I have not altered my way of life.

I didn't have to be shown some tragedy to be kind to my neighbor. I didn't need an attack on U.S. soil to move me to pray for the president and our country. I didn't need a wake up call to love my family more. I already love them and count the day's precious.

And I didn't need 9-11 to draw me to church, or to prompt me to be on my knees to seek God in prayer; it's just my way of life. No my life has not changed because of 9-11.

By Crystal A. Hinderer

Psalms 62:5 "My soul, wait thou only upon God, for my expectation is from Him."

Psalms 33:20 "Our soul waiteth for the Lord; He is our help and shield."

Psalms 118:8 "It is better to trust in the Lord than to put confidence in man."

Not Even For An Instant

Another day of grace, another day to pray for the lost. More souls to be saved, people can improve their life, and of course, avoid hell. But why do we pray for the lost? As Christians, we all most likely have unsaved we are praying for. We each have our own list of names with faces we can see in our mind. A neighbor, co-worker, boss, or relative; one person may have a poor life-style, and wouldn't it be great if their life got cleaned up.

A neighbor that doesn't act neighborly, or maybe you work with a very difficult co-worker. It would be wonderful if the person accepted Christ, and you could work together better.

Or possibly you have a relative that is just unapproachable. You might think that if the person were saved you would actually have something in common and could carry on a conversation.

God spoke to me the other day that He created us to worship and praise Him. And I need to pray for the lost to worship and praise Him. Not to be a better boss, not to have that warm family togetherness. Not to finally have that, "longed for" spiritual conversation with someone; to pray for the lost to worship and praise God. In the very instant I focus on my benefit, (although these desired thoughts may be well and good), I'm focusing on me and not God.

(1 Cor. 10; 31) "Whether therefore ye eat, or drink, or whatsoever ye do, do all to the glory of God." So now I pray for the lost in my life to come to know God to worship and praise Him. I'm trusting God that any flaws will fall away through God' perfect wisdom and timing. Once saved we all grow at different speeds. (Math. 7:1) "Judge not, that ye be not judged." It is my responsibility to love and pray for them; it is God's responsibility to convict and correct their life.

By Crystal A. Hinderer

John 3:30 "He must increase, but I must decrease."

To Pray The Bible Back To God

To pray the Bible back to God, to me, is the most perfect communication with God. Because even though I am imperfect, God's Word is.

"Likewise the Spirit also helpeth our infirmities, for we know not what we should pray for as we ought, but the Spirit itself maketh intercession for us with groanings which cannot be uttered. And he that searcheth the hearts knoweth what is the mind of the Spirit, because he maketh intercession for the saints according to the will of God" (Rom. 8:26-27).

Even when trying my best for God with the right motive, I am still in a sinful state. God takes my prayers and makes them all they should be. The Bible is perfect and I like to pray verses back to God. It strengthens me in my thoughts, and reassures me when speaking to God.

David encouraged himself in the Lord his God (1 Sam. 30:6). And David the king came and sat before the Lord (1 Chron. 17:6). King Hezekiah prayed before the Lord (2 Kings 19:15). These people and many more did not have the Bible; God spoke directly to them or through prophets. God speaks to us through His Word, and when we use Scripture to pray back to God it reinforces my faith because I know the Bible is true. The truth of the Word calms my fears, encourages my

21

heart, fades any doubt or worry, strengthens my spirit, and teaches me to trust God more. The Bible is truly the sword of the Spirit in the power of His might.

"But the Comforter, which is the Holy Ghost, whom the Father will send in my name, He shall teach you all things, and bring all things to your remembrance, whatsoever I have said unto you" (John 14:26).

I have to read the Bible to learn it and know it, and the Holy Spirit cannot bring to remembrance what I have not read in the first place.

By Crystal A. Hinderer

Psalms 119:11 "Thy Word have I hid in my heart that I might not sin against Thee."

The Torment Of Hell

In the story of the rich man and a beggar named Lazarus both died going to their eternal place. The rich man wanted to go back and warn his brothers, as he was now in hell and knew the reality of it. My mind flashed back to find this story in Scripture and read it once again (Luke 16: 19-31).

The news reported last week of putting a man to death for murder. His last words were in respect to Allah and my heart sank. What lies this man was told, and how sad he believed them. With his last breath he knew there was a heaven and a hell, and that he was lied to. He now knows there is only One True God.

As the rich man in the Bible story, I imagine all people wish they could pass from hell to warn family, friends, and even acquaintances about the reality of the torment of hell.

The Bible says that believers will have no tears or sorrow in heaven. I believe our Merciful Father will not allow us to remember our lost ones or else we'd grieve for them. We will only experience great joy. The rich man on the other hand wanted to warn his brothers, so he had a memory. I would think a memory would be a great torment as well. To remember those who had tried to lead them to Christ, but they repeatedly refused. To remember the many invitations for salvation they were offered, but rejected.

Satan is the father of lies and he continues everyday to take people to hell through lies (John 8:44). Satan tells people that they are not really so bad, and if one tries hard, gives money, or does good things they will make it to heaven. The Bible says in Ephesians 2:8-9 "For by grace are ye saved through faith; and that not of yourselves; it is the gift of God. Not of works, lest any man should boast."

Satan persuades people to think that all roads lead to heaven. The Holy Word says in John 14:6 "Jesus saith unto him, I am the way, the truth, and the life, no man cometh unto the Father, but by me."

Satan fools people into believing that once a person dies, they are just dead and put into the ground and that's all there is; so what does it matter anyway? He deceives some into believing that when they die and go to hell all of their friends will be there anyway; as if hell were going to be a fun place. Mathew 13:42 "And shall cast them into a furnace of fire; and there shall be wailing and gnashing of teeth."

Satan preys on others convincing them their life is so lost and past forgiveness, that God would never love them; nothing could be further from the Truth. Only the most unselfish love could send His only Son to a sinful, undeserving world. We have all been born lost, that is the very essence of why God sent His son. The greatest torment of hell will be the separation from God. The ultimate lie is to accept that God does not exist.

By Crystal A. Hinderer

Psalms 14:1 "The fool says in his heart, There is no God. They are corrupt, their deeds are vile; there is no one who does good."

Whatever It Takes

When we pray, "whatever it takes" for someone we know, God may use anything within His power to turn that life around to Him. "Turn thou us unto Thee, O Lord, and we shall be turned, renew our days as of old" (Lam. 5:21).

We do not pray for trials to happen to others, but we pray for God's will. Yet we know that God does use trials and situations to get peoples attention. But I do not think we have the right to pray, "whatever it takes" for someone else, unless we can pray that for our self.

Our Merciful Father in His wisdom knows that our pain is worth the suffering for the end result. Whether we would pray those words for our self or someone else, or not, the Father loves us too much to let us go our own way. And the Father is able, ready, and willing to do whatever it takes.

By Crystal A. Hinderer

Hebrews 12:6 "For whom the Lord loveth, He chasteneth and scourgeth every son whom He receiveth."

Hebrews 12:11 "No discipline seems pleasant at the time, but painful, Later on, however, it produces a harvest of righteousness and peace for those who have been trained by it."

Mustard Seed Faith

God can use faith as small as a mustard seed. I have thought of my faith like this too often, viewing it as small. But I was thinking of Saul who had no belief in Christ at all. Saul persecuted the disciples even unto death. He had men and women bound and put in prison. Saul breathed out threatenings and slaughter against the disciples of the Lord (Acts 9:1). The Lord stopped Saul on the road to Damascus (Acts 9:4) "...Saul, Saul, why persecutest thou me?"

I began to think that if the Lord could use Saul, who had hatred for the disciples, and had no regard for the Lord whatsoever, and Saul became a servant of Jesus Christ; could the Lord of course not use faith of a mustard seed? Could the Lord, not take willing heart of even the remotest faith, or the feeblest prayer? Or the faintest glimmer of the narrowest ray of light, and use that smallest portion of faith?

By Crystal A. Hinderer

Jeremiah 32:27 "Behold I am the Lord, the God of all flesh, is there anything too hard for me?"

Luke 1:27 "For with God nothing shall be impossible."

Luke 17:6 "And the Lord said, If ye had faith as a grain of mustard seed, ye might say unto this sycamine tree, Be thou plucked up by the root, and be thou planted in the sea, and it should obey you."

God Is God

This is just a page from my own life. It is not meant to lecture anyone in any way; for when we hurt the most, some people pour salt in our wounds as Job's so-called friends. This is written to just wrap my arms around people that hurt. I don't know if I can put into words what I wish I could say, because it is too much for even me to express to myself at times.

I cannot even really put my finger on a point in time of a date. But to say that one trial compounded into another. And each day of grief carried into the next with a rippling effect. It was an onslaught of trials that was so never-ending. One trial after another for years. I felt like we were in quicksand, afraid to move. There was just no breathing room.

Christians would talk about being strengthened by trials, but my husband and I did not feel strengthened, we felt beaten to death. I even had one dear Christian friend remark to me, "There is someone out there having a good time, because you must of got their trials too." My parents would shake their heads in unbelief, as if to say, "what next?"

I read in a Christian's office once, "Friends don't need it, and others will not believe it." Those are about the only words I've come a crossed (years later), to describe my husband

and I. We went through one thing right after another, and realized we just could not explain it to anyone; no one would believe it.

It truly seemed like Job, (in the regard that), before one messenger was finsished speaking, another was at the door. Even today I try not to look back because it still overwhelms me. The pain hurts too much, and I cry as if it were yesterday. But it was not yesterday, but many yesterdays. And yesterdays that are gone forever.

A rippling effect does not just touch one area. As a pebble into a pool, the pebble hits the water and forms a ring, which widens. So it was with our lives, but it wasn't one pebble, but many.

A broken down vehicle, or an illness, or being out of work, is more than just the initial problem. It is the rippling effect of the pebble in the pool, which in turn affects everything else.

It is deciding if you will buy auto insurance for the month, or feed your kids. It is deciding at some Christmases if you will get to bake, which you love, or buy food for the meal. It is deciding if you will go see your son play soccer, or use the money for gas to go to the doctor. And as pebbles kept hitting the pool, so came many more dividing decisions. Too many for me to handle, and too many tears.

For years I used to think that when I got to heaven I wanted God to open the books and explain it all to me. To explain what all the pebbles were for? So many pebbles with intertwining rings.

Through all the heartaches, setbacks, tears, and prayers, God has said to me. God is God. And God does not "owe" me an explanation. God is not "required" to explain His actions to me ever. I must just trust His wisdom and love for me.

By Crystal A. Hinderer

Isaiah 45:9 "Woe unto him that striveth with his Maker! Let the potsherd strive with the potsherds of the earth. Shall the clay say unto him that fashioneth it. What makest thou? Or thy work. He hath no hands."

Isaiah 43:7 "Even everyone that is called by my name, for I have created him for my glory, I have formed him, yea I have made him."

The One on one

Have you found the One on one? Do you set aside time with God, and for God? Going to church is needed. Group classes teach us. Fellowship is desired for us, (by God) for support, comfort, teaching, learning, giving, and sharing.

But have you found the One on one? If for some unforeseen reason your church building were gone today, would you still grow? Would you still read? Would you still have a lesson? Would you have time with God at all?

Years ago a dear Christian friend and prayer partner told me, (and I had to think on what she said) but she is right. She looked me square in the eyes and said "If I never stepped foot in any church again as long as I live, I wouldn't feel any closer to God than I do."

She wasn't saying, do not go to church. She wasn't saying we should be an island away from other Christians. Her closeness to God began in her heart, alone with God. Her closeness grew from the prayer times, alone with her Maker. Alone with her Bible to read and study, to give God her undivided attention. Alone to listen to all God had to say. And alone at times to be quiet and still, on her knees before

God, just to take in His presence. Have you found the One on one?

By Crystal A. Hinderer

Psalms 62:5 "My soul wait thou only upon God, for my expectation is from Him."

Just a Prelude

It was mixed emotions of sadness and joy at the funeral, and grieving with the family in their loss. The emptiness would remain long after the funeral was over. The tears and heavy hearts would longer to cling unwelcomely through days of mourning. But there was also a calmness of inner peace.

There were so many Christians there I had not seen in a long time for one reason or another. And even though the day was one of great sorrow, there was a gladness to see each other again, and to share renewed hugs and smiles.

I began to think of heaven and what a joy we Christians will have one day, and even so much the more so. People we haven't seen for so long, and possibly some we've even forgotten about through the years.

But not to just think of friends and loved ones in heaven, but also people to meet for the first time that we've never met but have prayed for. I really began to be overwhelmed inside with the Lord's presence. Though not saying a word out loud the Lord and I were consciously talking with each other, as I looked around at all the faces. The feeling inside was so strange, yet real.

In my dictionary it reads that "prelude" is something preceding and preparing for more important matters. I like that word and definition, for our lives are preparing now on earth, for more important matters in heaven.

That close inner feeling of seeing old friends, and the peace of knowing we'd all be in heaven together was just a prelude to the eternal joy we will share in heaven. Just think of all Christians together before God and Christ. All Christians from all over the world to come on bended knees to worship and praise The Savior.

By Crystal A. Hinderer

Romans 12; 15 "Rejoice with them that do rejoice, and weep with them that weep."

Sometimes

In the stillness of the morning the Lord and I meet together and my heart reaches for Him. Sometimes to come on bended knees, just to silently wait. Without speaking a word. Without asking for anything. Without tears of some trial or heartache. Without even interceding for another. Just to be quiet and still, to listen for what God needs to say to me. To wait on Him, just to take in His presence.

> Sometimes no sound be ever muttered
> Or word be ever said
> To sit quietly before You
> Is my daily bread
>
> And the silence is rewarding
> As my soul awaits on Thee
> For the beauty of your presence
> Between You and me

By Crystal A. Hinderer

Psalms 62:5 "My soul wait thou only upon God, for my expectation is from Him."

Psalms 42:1 "As the hart panteth after the water brooks, so panteth my soul after Thee, O God."

My First Love

It is so easy for me to be carried away with writing. With reading The Word, looking up meanings in our Bible directory, and jotting down thoughts. Putting lines and thoughts together for the paragraphs in order. Seeing another finished article all typed on crisp paper is exciting to me. And in my life, being a Christian from youth, I have pretty much written to God, and about God, or His ways.

The other day I was reflecting how I used to write many years ago. At that point in time of my life, God would often wake me up in the middle of the night, to offer me the opportunity to write about Him; it was wonderful

I was reading Rev. 2:1-4 the other day. The church at Ephesus did so many good things. They labored without fainting, had patience, and did not like evil, yet they lost their first love. They were busy doing things for God, but lost their love with God.

Studying that portion of Scripture, I realized I had been guilty of that sin without even realizing it. Years ago I was getting up to write about God, and the excitement of writing about God, and the thrill of writing. But I wasn't getting up to seek God to be with Him; and there is a huge difference. I had to ask God for forgiveness for my lack of knowledge in this, and He did, and we cried together. Tears of forgiveness, and tears of joy that I learned something new.

My writing is not more important than my time alone with God. The fellowship of the praise, prayer, and reading The Word, is more important than writing about Him. God is already complete without me. God must be my first love and passion. My writing is just an extension of that First Love.

By Crystal A. Hinderer

Mark 12:30 "And thou shalt love the Lord thy God with all thy heart, and with all thy soul, and with all thy mind, and with all thy strength: this is the first commandment."

Before I Even Asked

Again Lord, even though looking unto You, I was limiting You, by looking to You through my eyes. I need to look to You through your eyes. Enlarge my borders I said, prayed, and meant, and You did in 2001. And I was saying not if but how? So I believed You could.

I've been thinking that when I have witnessed, by sharing the gospel message; I thought in terms of passing out tracts to evangelize. Thinking in terms of what I thought You wanted and expected of me, to reach people for You.

Then my mind remembers Isaiah, and I find it in chapter 55:8-9. "For my thoughts are not your thoughts, neither are your ways my ways, saith the Lord. For as the heavens are higher than the earth, so are my ways higher than your ways, and my thoughts than your thoughts."

One of the things that amazes me is that when I seek God to focus on Him and for Him to give Him my all, He turns it around to bless me; as if to reward me for what I should be doing anyway.

Enlarge my coasts, the borders of my world. Sometimes I see my world as small, forgetting I have a great God with limitless boundaries and resources. Before I even asked God to enlarge my coasts in 2001, He knew my desire in 2003.

"For there is not a word in my tongue, but, lo, O Lord, thou knowest it altogether" (Ps. 139:4). "Commit thy works unto the Lord, and thy thoughts shall be established" (Prov. 16:3). "Delight thyself also in the Lord, and He shall give thee the desires of thine heart" (Ps. 37:4).

In seeking You Lord with my desire You have already turned it around to enlarge my coasts, to bless me. As if to reward me again, to build me up, to strengthen and encourage others. Except it really isn't me at all. "How precious also are thy thoughts unto me, O God! How great is the sum of them!" (Ps. 139:7).

By Crystal A. Hinderer

Job 32:8 "But there is a spirit in man, and the inspiration of the Almighty giveth them understanding."

John 3:27 "John answered and said, A man can receive nothing, except it be given him from heaven."

1 Cor. 2:5 "That your faith should not stand in the wisdom of men, but in the power of God."

Phil. 1:6 "Being confident of this very thing, that he which hath begun a good work in you will perform it until the day of Jesus Christ."

To Inquire Of God

In 2002 I committed to reading The Bible through; I had never done that before. I challenge anyone to take up this goal, it is greatly rewarding.

I like not only reading the Word, but also studying it. One of the things I took note of was enquiring of God. It may not sound like much, but I think it is of great importance. Yea sure, Christians pray and ask things of God in prayer or pray for others, but I mean to inquire of God. To ask God His direction for my life. Ask God's view of how to handle situations beforehand. Ask God's desire for my life even though I have good motives. Just because something is a Christ centered thought or ambition, doesn't mean it is where God wants me to be. To ask Him for my daily direction, everyday.

The God of All, who made the creation and put everything in motion, knows me better than anyone. "My substance was not hid from Thee, when I was made in secret, and curiously wrought in the lowest parts of the earth" (Ps. 139:15). Why should I not ask God what is best for me? Why should I not seek God's decisions for my life? Why should I not pray and inquire of God, and then take the time to wait for His leading, and answers for me? Why should I not invite Him into every area of my life?

43

To point out how serious God views our not asking Him, I came across 1 Chron. 10:13-14. "So Saul died for his transgression which he committed against the Lord, even against the Word of the Lord, which he kept not, and also for asking counsel of one that had a familiar spirit, to inquire of it; <u>And inquired not of the Lord</u>, therefore he slew him, and turned the kingdom unto David the son of Jesse." (Isaiah 30:1) "Woe to the rebellious children, saith the Lord, <u>that take counsel, but not of me;</u> and that cover with a covering, but not of my spirit, that they may add sin to sin." (Isaiah 31:1)"Woe to them that go down to Egypt for help; and stay on horses, and trust in chariots, because they are many, and in horsemen, because they are very strong; <u>but they look not unto the Holy One of Israel, neither seek the Lord!</u>"

It's not only wise to inquire of God, but respectful. It is an honor to highly regard God's authority in my life. Someone who loved me so much to send His only Son to die for me, so I could be in heaven with Him forever, certainly cares deeply for the details of my daily life on earth now.

By Crystal A. Hinderer

Mathew 7:11 "If ye then, being evil know how to give good gifts unto your children, how much more shall your Father which is in heaven give good things to them that ask Him?"

Sorrow And Joy

I attended the funeral of an eight-year-old boy, whose parents and grandparents are Christians. Being a Christian too, it was mixed emotions of course. All were grieving with the family as Romans 12:15 says, " weep with them that weep." Sadness for the lives so suddenly interrupted by their loss. All the adjustmentments that would come. My mind ran through many things. Lord we are so fragile in your hands. We can be here one minute, and gone the next.

The church was packed, and the message in honor of the child's passing was sincere and truthful. For yes, we Christians grieve over the loss of our loved ones, but we also rejoice. Romans 12:15 also says "Rejoice with them that do rejoice…" We rejoice in knowing our Christian loved ones are in heaven. We rejoice to know their sufferings and sorrows are gone forever. We have glad hearts in knowing we will see them again one day in heaven. Christians have joy in the truth that we have eternal life after death. We have a hope beyond all measure to take us through tough times. I cannot imagine life without God in this world. Even the thought of life without God, and all that involves, is painful to think about.

The toughest times I have ever faced would be nothing compared to struggling through this world without Christ in my life. All the tears He's wiped away, and strength supporting me at just the right moments in my life. All the words of comfort to my soul when I have felt overwhelmed. The many times His gentle hands lifted me up out of despair. The times He set my feet on the right path. Life without God would be the greatest sorrow I could ever face. It is truly the greatest sorrow and regret; those who reject God will ever know, forever.

Christians definitely are not excused from trials and struggles in life. We have many sorrows and heartaches to face in this world. But the peace of being a Christian, and the thankfulness to God for His gift of His Son, far outweighs the sorrow. I cannot thank God enough for Him being in my life every day. Just knowing God, is the greatest joy.

By Crystal A. Hinderer

2 Corin. 4:17 "For our light affliction, which is but for a moment, worketh for us a far more exceeding and eternal weight of glory."

God Is The Reality Of My Expectation

In my life, all that was, and is, and shall be
Lord is You

The things in life I wanted
But learned to give up
For You told me they were not needed

The ideas and thoughts I held so highly in view
Have faded
To make room for You

To understand, to open my hands
From so tightly holding things around me in life
That it is not letting go or loosing
Because then, You fill my hands abundantly
With more than I could hold

continued

To know that You are changing me
To more than I could ever be
To fulfill in me
More than I had ever desired

And to know that the center of it all
Always comes back to You

By Crystal A. Hinderer

Psalms 62:5 "My soul wait thou only upon God, for my expectation is from Him."

Merciful Father

God is longsuffering. With each tornado, flood, famine, hurricane, or earthquake around the world. Some people look God as some destroyer, or hand of doom, but God is The Living God of love and mercy. Out of the fierceness of each disaster, there is still God's gentle enduring love. God has patient waiting, to give people another opportunity to receive Christ.

Each plague in Exodus was carried out to the final plague of the death of each firstborn in Egypt of man and beast (Ex. 12:29). But with each plague there could have a turning point for anyone to repent to God. Each individual has a free choice and a free will. Even during the plagues God gave people a choice. "He that feared the word of the Lord among the servants of Pharaoh made his servants and cattle flee in the houses. And he that regarded not the word of the Lord left his servants and his cattle in the field" (Ex.9: 20-21).

We may be the on-looker with hopeful waiting for one we are praying for to receive salvation. But God is the Merciful Father, waiting with longsuffering for that one to come into His arms through His Son. God is the One longing to give the only hope for their soul. Yearning for their fellowship and desiring they receive Christ. God longs for us to know the joy of His forgiveness, the freedom repentance brings, and His deep abiding Love.

Yes, we have disasters, and threats of war upon our nation, and fighting, and unrest throughout the world; the Bible said it would happen. But these are not just happenings; they are also progressive warnings and opportunities of grace. Warnings as God gives one more day of grace to the lost, and warnings that the time is short. Opportunities for Christians to pray and witness to a lost world. Opportunities to share the message of Christ with those around us, and to get our lives in order.

God is not unkind; on the contrary, God is patiently waiting with longsuffering as a wise and merciful Father.

By Crystal A. Hinderer

1 Cor. 1:3 "Blessed be God, even the Father of our Lord Jesus Christ, the Father of mercies and the God of all comfort."

2 Peter 3:9 "The Lord is not slack concerning His promise, as some men count slackness; but is long-suffering to us-ward, not willing that any should perish; but that all should come to repentance."

More Than Words

With each story there is a lesson God is teaching me. Something God needs to say to me. I've heard people say they wonder where God is, or if there is a God at all. I say there is a God, the Living God, and all one has to do to find God is to seek him. And if anyone wants to hear him, all they have to do is learn to listen.

God speaks in so many ways. In sunsets, and early morning hours. In fresh breezes, and rays of sunshine outlining clouds. He speaks through the voices of people in word or song, the Holy Bible, and on lines of ink of others. But make no mistake, God speaks. And if you truly seek God he will be found, and he will even answer. (Jer. 33:3)"Call unto me, and I will answer thee, and show thee great and mighty things, which thou knowest not." (Jer. 29:13) "And ye shall seek me, and find me, when ye shall search for me with all your heart."

As I write, I'm thinking of just what is the essence of what I write and why? What I want others to see is Christ the Savior and God, and his hand still at work in the world today. For people to focus more deeply on God. To know his presence is real, and that God is the Living God; not just the

God, "heard of" in stories long ago; but also the God of here and now. I want people to feel what I write.

My writing began as pouring out my heart to The One who knows me best. It took on the form of communication between God and I, to realizing to use my gift for him, instead of just writing about him. And I love to encourage people for God.

We all mess up in one way or another. People need to feel arms around them hugging them. All too often when we are hurting, people pour salt in our wounds, just like Job's so-called friends. I want people to see that we all mess up, and I want to give people hugs right off the pages.

Some of us do not come from the perfect Christian family. Some of us don't have the perfect marriage with the perfect kids, because we are not perfect our self in a less than perfect world.

I am never glad about my sins; God does not like any sin. Jesus Christ thankfully died for all sin, even mine. But it is also my flaws that return me to my knees again and again. Praying to my God, and having gratitude for salvation for one like me.

So I must write because I have stories to tell, lessons to learn, and praises to sin out. And it is more than words, with each life encouraged, any heart that is lifted, and every voice that can praise again or anew. Any person that is strengthened, to strengthen another, by encouraging desire, for anyone to refocus more deeply on God. It is far more than words to me, it is my little corner of the world reaching out to a sinful and hurting world, saying we all mess up. But God is so ready to forgive, because Jesus paid the price for all our sins, with more than words.

By Crystal A. Hinderer

52

Ps. 19:14 "Let the words of my mouth, and the meditation of my heart, be acceptable in they sight, O Lord, my strength and my Redeemer."

The God Of Here And Now

L ord you are so much more, so vast, so inexhaustible, you are beyond. So far beyond the stories of long ago. You are the Ancient of Days, you are before, and so high above.

You walked in the Garden of Eden, you created it. People remember hearing about Adam and Eve, the Garden of Eden, and the disobedience. But you are beyond that. It was more than a story, it was You, creating life, to give love to man, to know you and walk with you. Adam sinned and there was a need for the world to seek you, accept you, and abide in you.

You spoke through Noah, and there was a flood. But You are so much more than a story about water flooding the earth, and animals two by two. You are Faithfulness to those who love and obey you. You are Hope to those that listen. You are a Father that sees the need to spare man from himself. You are a new Beginning.

The plagues of Egypt were very real; The Bible does not lie. People through generations have turned away from you, but that does not invalidate the story or the meaning. You are so much more than a story about plagues. You are Patience in waiting for people to turn. You are a loving Father with

55

longsuffering. You are Eagerness to forgive. You are Hope to those that listen. You are a Father that longs to spare man from himself. You are the Journey of each life.

Christ became a baby and lived on earth as man. He did miracles and taught many. He was tempted, physically depleted, ridiculed and mocked. The story of Christ's life goes on to the Cross, Resurrection, and sitting at the right hand of God. But you are so much more than a story of your life. You were God-man to feel our pains. You performed miracles to enlighten people to believe in you. You died to save the world, and accomplish what God designed. And you sit at the right hand of God bestowed in all your glory. You are the Perfect Gift from the Father, offering man a choice. You are Love in Waiting.

Today we have world disasters, wars, unrest, and threats of attacks. Broken homes, diseases, abused children, and abortion for convenience. But you reach far beyond current events. You are so much more than the story of today. You are Mercy, giving opportunities for people to turn to you. Some will always reject you, but that does not invalidate your existence and the meaning. You are Hope to those that listen. You are the loving Father to provide a way for the world. You are the Way, the Truth, and the Life. You are the Never-Ending Story.

By Crystal A. Hinderer

Romans 5:1-2 "Therefore being justified by faith, we have peace with God through our Lord Jesus Christ. By whom also we have access by faith into this grace wherein we stand, and rejoice in hope of God."

So Much More

Easter is almost here, and my paper is blank. One of the most important days of the year and how can I have nothing written. So I pause, to think just what Easter does mean to me.

Christ died for my sins and rose again, finishing the work on the cross. Sometimes I think how can there even be words enough to express gratitude forever, for such an unmerited gift.

Salvation is the greatest gift in the world, and the most important decision anyone can make. Yet salvation is so much more than a decision to accept Christ, for Easter does not stop at the cross. Once a person accepts Christ, it is a lifelong journey. It is forever having the presence of God. It is the indwelling Holy Spirit to lead and direct daily. It is answers to prayer in remarkable ways that never ceases to amaze me.

It is peace through sorrows, and total forgiveness. It is a deep inner joy, and strength to sustain trials. It is undeserved mercy, and mended hearts. It is freedom from death, and an eternal home in heaven.

It is determination to please God through love and obedience, and overwhelmed happiness when I do. It is

God restructuring my life better than I ever imagined. And a deeper meaning to everything around me.

Easter is so much more than Christ dying on a cross. Easter and salvation are just the beginning. The cross reaches far beyond its remembrance of one day of the year. Christ died for the sins of the world, and rose again so we could have life. If only we would become so much more.

By Crystal A. Hinderer
Butch L. Hinderer

John 10:10 "The thief cometh not, but for to steal, and to kill, and to destroy, I am come that they might have life, and that they might have it more abundantly."

Only In A Whisper

The more I walk with Christ, the more I depend upon Him. My situations are becoming more of what God is doing, than what's happening. Knowing God is definitely never boring, regardless of what some think of God or Christianity. God never ceases to amaze me. Prayers are answered in remarkable ways that could only be God's timing and purpose. It is truly wonderful to begin to realize how much God does love, and really has my life under control, in spite of me.

Recently I was thinking I' would like two more Bibles; a small one for the car when I needed it, and an N.I.V. The church we attend now use the N.I.V. a great deal. I was raised with the King James Version, but I've been wanting to compare for my personal study.

My daughter took me with her to a yard sale the other day. I purchased a large box of kids story books in great condition for $3.00. I carted the box home to get a better look at my treasure. To my surprise, there were two Bibles underneath all the books. A small New Testament in the King James Version, which is now in the car, and a New Testament N.I.V.

As I sat looking at the two Bibles, I could only cry to experience God's hand of giving to me personally. It was the Lord showing me how much He cares for me, and the details of my life. And as a Christian, I do not believe in coincidence. I was overwhelmed by God's personal attention to me.

The Bible says in Mathew 7:11 "If ye then, being evil, know how to give good gifts unto your children, how much more shall your Father which is in heaven give good things to them that ask him?" But I hadn't even asked; it was only the whisper of a passing thought. I am only one person in this great big world; but the Father cares.

And I began to consider. If God cares about two more Bibles for me, just from a passing thought, how much more readily does God hear the earnest prayers I pray? How much more is God moved when I speak intercessions for others? And how intently are His eyes fixed upon those that deeply search for him.

By Crystal A. Hinderer

Jer. 29:13 "And ye shall seek me, and find me, when ye shall search for me with all your heart."

Eph. 3; 20 "Now unto him that is able to do exceeding abundantly above all that we ask or think, according to the power that worketh in us,"

Finding God

The Bible is truly the Living Word that never grows stale or lies dormant. It is alive for each generation. Every time its pages are searched and sought it sheds new light. I loved hearing Bible stories when I was young. Daniel and the lion's den, Samson and Goliath, Noah's ark, Jonah and the whale, the baby Jesus born in Bethlehem, and many more. I was always taken to church, attended VBS, and taught to pray, to which I am eternally thankful. I had an awareness of God, Jesus, and the Bible early in life. I prayed to Jesus, but I was afraid of God.

Jesus died for me, was closer than a brother, and was born as a baby to live and die for the sins of the world. Jesus also walked among the people, healed the sick and had compassion. It always seemed easy to love Him.

When I was young I had also heard of the Trinity. The idea of the Holy Spirit was a little hard to comprehend; yet I tried to accept this even though I did not fully understand it. But there was still the matter of God, and He scared me.

God in my mind was a strict disciplinarian who could send hail and fire to the earth if He so desired as in Exodus 10, or any other plague. And I knew I was not perfect. In 1 Chronicles 13 a man named Uzza put his hand to the ark to steady it when the oxen stumbled and God smote Uzza. I always felt bad for Uzza trying to do a good thing it seemed. So I tried to watch my steps in life.

"And when the people complained, it displeased the Lord, and the Lord heard it, and His anger was kindled; and the fire of the Lord burnt among them, and consumed them that were in the uttermost parts of the camp" (Numbers 11:1).

In 2 Samuel chapter 24 David numbered the people putting confidence in the strength of the number instead of God's hand. 70,000 men died of a pestilence even though this was David's sin and not theirs.

Exodus 19:12-13 explains how boundaries had to be placed around Mt. Sinai, and if anyone touched even the border of the mountain they were to be put to death. When I was a child I was aware of God, but did not call to Him. I felt I should keep my distance so I would talk to Jesus.

Jesus Christ became my Savior when I was 16, but it was not until years later that I found God. Through attending church and Bible study I was drawn to want to know God. I needed to know Jesus' Father in heaven that Jesus loved so much. I determined to seek God early making time for Him with the first fruits of my day. I determined to read the Bible through, which I had never done before. The more I sought God the more the words in the Bible would take on new meaning. In my search Daniel 10:12 spoke too me. "Then said he unto me, Fear not, Daniel, for from the first day that thou didst set thine heart to understand, and to chasten thyself before thy God, thy words were heard, and I am come for thy words." That verse touched my heart.

How beautiful I thought that God in heaven took time for personal attention to Daniel. I began to see God not as a strict disciplinarian, but the caring Heavenly Father who loves me. God's boundaries, whether around the border of a mountain or the instructions for my life are there to protect me.

I wanted God to come for my words, whether spoken in my heart or written on lines of ink. I wanted God to know me, and to know my name, and I wanted God to be pleased with my life before Him. I found in the Bible that God always knew me and everything about me, even before I was ever born. And God knows the number of my days and the searching of my life.

God's best is for me to know Him. To acknowledge who God is and worship Him in humble adoration and praise. God is sovereign. "Thine, O Lord, is the greatness, and the power, and the glory, and the victory, and the majesty; for all that is in the heaven and in the earth is Thine; Thine is the kingdom, O Lord, and Thou art exalted as head above all.

(12) Both riches and honor come of Thee, and Thou reignest over all; and in Thine hand is power and might; and in Thine hand it is to make great, and to give strength unto all" (1 Chron.29: 11-12).

It is an honored privilege to fellowship with the Living God. To stand in awe of His greatness and know His love still cares for every detail of my life. God always desired to give me His best; He was just patiently waiting for me to find Him.

By Crystal A. Hinderer

1 Corinthians 13:11 "When I was a child, I spake as a child, I understood as a child, I thought as a child; but when I became a man, I put away childish things."

Out Of The Equation

S ome people want prayer out of schools and out of all public functions. Others say that a baby is not a life at conception. Many try to discredit God as the Creator of creation, explaining that people evolved from monkeys. Others do not want to hear The Pledge of Allegiance because it states "under God". And some think The Holy Bible is not real but only a book of man-made stories. Oh the foolishness of man.

God is the source of all life, majesty, mercy, wisdom, and hope. There is nothing of value without God, and no purpose for anything without him.

It does not matter what occupation a person chooses, baker, housewife, teacher, doctor, ditch-digger, or scientist. If a person refuses Jesus Christ as their Savior they miss the whole reason for their existence. They miss why they were born and the deeper knowledge that only God can give.

A scientist may know all about atoms, protons, and neutrons, but unless that person understands the greatness of who God is in the scheme of things, his understanding is small in reality to God. It is the same for anyone, whether a person digs ditches or works in the White House. When anyone refuses Jesus Christ as their Savior they miss the most important knowledge of all.

People were created to love and worship God. Whether a person accepts Jesus Christ as their Savior or not, does not diminish God at all or his sovereignty. Because people do not believe the Bible, it is not less valid or true. People cannot sever God from creation, God made the earth and universe and all there is. (Jeremiah 10:12) "He hath made the earth by his power, he hath established the world by his wisdom, and hath stretched out the heavens by his discretion." God is much higher than man and is before all things. "All things were made by him, and without him was not anything made that was made" (John 1:3).

Man's wisdom is foolish to try to take God or even his name out of the picture. Man cannot erase God out of the equation, God is the Equation.

By Crystal A. Hinderer

1 Cor. 1:18-20 "For the preaching of the cross is to them that perish foolishness; but unto us which are saved it is the power of God.

For it is written, I will destroy the wisdom of the wise, and will bring to nothing the understanding of the prudent.

Where is the wise? Where is the scribe? Where is the disputer of this world? Hath not God made foolish the wisdom of this world?"

God-Bumps

Some people get goose bumps but not me, I get God-bumps. Some consider God antiquated, but I know God is alive and well and very real in my life. God is mysterious and distant for his thoughts are higher than our thoughts and his ways passed finding out. Yet the heavenly Father is always watching his own and constantly caring for them closely.

God is definitely alive and it is with great respect to reach for him, but I am even more awestruck when God reaches back, and he does. God loves when we delight in him. God not only speaks if we listen, but he will wrap his arms around you and let you know he is ever so near.

God never ceases to amaze me, and I write that a lot but it is so true. I thank God often that he and I communicate through writing and words. I love to express my heart on paper to God, even though my words are less than adequate for all God is, and even with my feebleness of pen when I praise him he blesses me. I falter and struggle in life yet God makes himself known with personal attention of loving caresses around my heart right where I live and breathe, in my passion to write.

It is not about me or because of me, and I certainly do not hold myself up above others. God is no respecter of persons, he loves all sinners. I don't have an inside track or some secret code in a prayer; God and I just walk and talk a lot. God has grown very dear to me; it took me years to find him. I knew Jesus but not God, and now that I have found him I just enjoy being with him.

Often after writing a story I will read in my daily devotional, or hear in our pastor's message an exact word or thought I just wrote about, and that always astonishes me. In that moment it causes me to pause and God just floods my soul with his presence. It is a special blessing from God to me, graciously given but never deserved. No there is no audible voice, or hand writing on the wall, but like a gentle breeze you cannot see, yet you know its there, I hear God undeniably speak.

By Crystal A. Hinderer

Psalms 46:10 "Be still and know that I am God, I will be exalted among the heathen, I will be exalted in the earth."

Jer. 29:13 "And ye shall seek me and find me, when ye shall search for me with all your heart."

My Inspiration

Thank you to you God just doesn't seem enough, and where do I begin? Of course to thank you for sending your only Son to die for me. Salvation is the greatest gift but there is so much more. To thank you is so deep and broad and forever.

For the pardon of sins and mercy bestowed. To thank you for your watchful eye upon me, and your constant care. Your presence ever near, and your love holding me.

You nudge me to try like a mother bird gently pushing her young out of the nest. You encourage my life to keep on with the positives, as you have loved me through the negatives.

You inspire me to grow by simply drawing me to yourself. I would not be who I am, or think like I do, or write what is on my heart without you.

You bless me as I praise you, and you give me more than I could ever write into words. You are the praise of my life and my great inspiration. I thank you for new beginnings, got you truly enable me to fly.

By Crystal A. Hinderer

Mathew 6:21 "For where your treasure is, there will your heart be also."

JAH

Lord to awake each morning and say my first "hello and good morning" to you. To acknowledge who you are and who you are in my life. You are God.

You are the Hope of my daily living, the Joy of my heart, the Rock I depend upon, and the Hiding Place that no one sees.

You are the Counselor that gives me the truth I need to hear. You are my Refuge from life's storms, and the Candle to light my path. You are my Gratitude of praise, the Inspiration of my words, and the Friend I confide in.

You are the Voice that called me, the Cross that saved me, the Door that opened, the Shepherd that leads me, and the Love that enfolds me.

You are my Deepest Desire and the Longing in my soul. You are far away upon your throne where only you deserve to be; and yet you abide within my heart.

You are the Keeper of the universe, and the Keeper of my soul. You are the Giver of every breath I take. Your palm is the pillow for my head and your wings cover me in the night. You are the only Living God, and you are my God.

By Crystal A. Hinderer

71

Ps. 145:18 "The Lord is nigh unto all them that call upon him, to all that call upon him in truth."

Ps. 68:4 "Sing unto God, sing praises to his name, extol him that rideth upon the heavens, by his name JAH, and rejoice before him."

Ps. 34:1 "I will bless the Lord at all times, his praise shall continually be in my mouth."

Ps. 91:4 "He shall cover thee with his feathers, and under his wings shalt thou trust; his truth shall be thy shield and buckler."

Ps. 63:7 "Because thou hast been my help, therefore in the shadow of thy wings will I rejoice."

Ps. 61:4 "I will abide in thy tabernacle for ever, I will trust in the covert of thy wings. Selah."

Printed in the United States
64757LVS00002B/1-273